VALERIAN AND LAURELINE

THE EMPIRE OF A THOUSAND PLANETS

J.-C. MÉZIÈRES AND P. CHRISTIN
COLOUR WORK: E. TRANLÉ

9th CINEBOOK
The 9th Art Publisher

Original title: Valerian 2 – L'empire des mille planètes
Original edition: © Dargaud Paris, 1971 by Christin, Mezières & Tran-Lê
First published in *Pilote* magazine in 1969
www.dargaud.com
All rights reserved
English translation: © 2011 Cinebook Ltd
Translator: Jerome Saincantin
Lettering and text layout: Imadjinn
This edition first published in Great Britain in 2011 by
Cinebook Ltd
56 Beech Avenue
Canterbury, Kent
CT4 7TA
www.cinebook.com
Fourth printing: December 2016
Printed in Spain by EGEDSA
A CIP catalogue record for this book
is available from the British Library
ISBN 978-1-84918-087-0

9th CINEBOOK
The 9th Art Publisher

DARK, INFINITE EXPANSE OF THE UNIVERSE...
BLAZING SUNS BATHING UNKNOWN LANDS IN LIGHT...
HOW MANY BILLIONS OF CIVILISATIONS,
HOW MANY BILLIONS UPON BILLIONS OF BEINGS
MIGHT CALL YOU HOME?...

IN A DISTANT PART OF
THE GALAXY, ONE PLANET IS
THE HEART OF A HUGE SOLAR
SYSTEM.
        IT IS
SYRTE THE MAGNIFICENT,
CAPITAL OF THE EMPIRE OF
A THOUSAND PLANETS.

SYRTE AND ITS FABULOUS
IMPERIAL PALACE ARE HOME
TO THE LAST MEMBER OF A
DYNASTY THAT HAS RULED
OVER ALL THE SYSTEM'S
PLANETS SINCE TIME
IMMEMORIAL.

ONLY THE PRINCE'S
FAVOURITES AND AMBASSADORS
ACCREDITED BY IMPERIAL
AUTHORITIES EVER ENTER
THE HEAVILY GUARDED PALACE.
THE PEOPLE, OFTEN GATHERED
AT THE DOORSTEP OF
THE BUILDING, HEAR BUT
THE ECHOES OF MYSTERIOUS
CELEBRATIONS...

BUT SYRTE IS, FIRST OF ALL,
THE GREATEST MARKET OF
THE EMPIRE. IN ITS SOUQS,
ARRAYED ALONG THE CANALS,
ONE CAN FIND ANYTHING.
THE MERCHANT GUILD ROAMS
THE SYSTEM TO BRING BACK
COUNTLESS WONDERS...

... HYPNOTIC SCHAMIRS FROM PLANET GLIMIUS, INSIDE OF WHICH ONE SLEEPS TO FIND OBLIVION...

... LIVING STONES OF ARPHAL THAT STICK TO ONE'S SKIN TO MAKE THE MOST BEAUTIFUL JEWELS...

... EXCEEDINGLY RARE TELEPATHIC SPIGLICS FROM BLUXTE — PETS THAT LIVE ON THEIR MASTERS' HEADS AND COMMUNICATE TO THEM THEIR CONSTANT BLISS...

... RARE METALS, EXOTIC DELICACIES, MULTICOLOURED FABRICS... IN THE LABYRINTH OF SYRTE'S STREETS, A POPULATION COMING FROM ALL PLANETS BUYS, SELLS, SOMETIMES STEALS...

ONE ALSO COMES TO SYRTE TO CONSULT WITH THE ENLIGHTENEDS, HEALERS OF THE BODY AND SEERS OF THE SOUL, INSCRUTABLE WITHIN THEIR METAL HELMETS...

... IT IS SAID THAT THEIR POWER KEEPS GROWING, AND SOME BELIEVE THAT THEY MAY HAVE BECOME THE TRUE MASTERS OF SYRTE. FEW IN NUMBERS, THE ENLIGHTENEDS ARE THE MOST RESPECTED— AND, ABOVE ALL, THE MOST FEARED—GUESTS OF THE PALACE...

... WHEN THEY'RE NOT LIVING INSIDE THEIR TEMPLE-FORTRESSES, DEEP IN THE SYRTIAN JUNGLES.

FINALLY, SYRTE IS ALSO A GIGANTIC SPACEPORT. SINCE THE FIRST DAYS OF INTER-PLANETARY TRAVEL, IT HAS WELCOMED SHIPS FROM ALL OVER THE SOLAR SYSTEM. THERE'S NO CUSTOMS, NO SECURITY... ONE COMES TO SYRTE THE MAGNIFICENT UNRESTRAINED, AND ONE LEAVES IT FREELY...

AND HEAVY TRADE VESSELS AS WELL AS LIGHT CRAFTS PEACEFULLY PLY THE SEA ROUTES BETWEEN THE BACK COUNTRY, THE CAPITAL AND THE SPACEPORT. PROPELLED BY THEIR SOLAR SAILS—ON THIS WINDLESS PLANET—THE BOATS THRONG THE CANALS...

AND YET, DESPITE ITS AGE AND GLORY, SYRTE ISN'T WHAT IT ONCE WAS... EVERYWHERE, ABANDONED RUINS, COLLAPSED SEAWALLS AND SILTED-UP HARBOURS...

THE IMPERIAL PALACE ITSELF IS INCREASINGLY RUNDOWN...

IN THE JUNGLE, WHERE POOR FISHERMEN HUNT THE DANGEROUS MARCYAM—A GIGANTIC WATER SNAKE—FOR ITS PRECIOUS SKIN...

... ONLY THE ENLIGHTENEDS' IMPREGNABLE TEMPLES CONTRAST WITH THE GENERAL POVERTY.

IN SPACE, A FEW LIGHT-YEARS AWAY FROM SYRTE...

6

YOU CAN START RECORDING. IT'S READY.

RIGHT. HI, KIDS! THIS IS VALERIAN, SHIP NUMBER XB982; WE LEFT GALAXITY FOR THE SYRTIAN SYSTEM ON THE 23RD OF SEPTEMBER, 2720...

ORAL REPORT NUMBER FOUR. WE ARE NOW IN THE VICINITY OF SYRTE AND HAVE RECOVERED THE LAST OF THE TERRAN AUTOMATIC PROBES THAT PRECEDED OUR OWN ARRIVAL. AS PLANNED, THE RECORDINGS OF SYRTIAN SPEECH ALLOWED US TO LEARN THE COMMON LANGUAGE BY HYPNO-TEACHING. WE'RE ABOUT TO MAKE THE LAST SPACE/TIME JUMP AND LAND AT SYRTE'S SPACEPORT. NOTHING MUCH TO REPORT FOR THE MOMENT—OVER!

HMM... I DON'T REALLY KNOW, LAURELINE! ANYWAY, WE'RE JUST AGENTS OF THE SPATIO-TEMPORAL SERVICE. OUR JOB IS TO ASSESS WHETHER SYRTE IS A DANGER TO EARTH—OR COULD BECOME ONE...

IT'S A STRANGE FEEL-ING... TO THINK WE'RE ABOUT TO MAKE CONTACT WITH THE FIRST GREAT GALACTIC CIVILISATION OVER WHICH EARTH HAS HAD NO INFLUENCE! DO YOU THINK THERE'S ANY ACTUAL DANGER?

BUT EVERYTHING SEEMS TO INDICATE THAT SYRTE HASN'T DISCOVERED THE SPACE/TIME JUMP! IF THEIR PEOPLE HAVEN'T SPREAD OUTSIDE OF THEIR SYSTEM, IT'S BECAUSE INTERPLANETARY TRAVEL STILL RELIES ON CONVENTIONAL PROPULSION. TO REACH ANOTHER STAR, THE SYRTIANS WOULD HAVE TO TRAVEL FOR CENTURIES.

I KNOW THAT! MAYBE THERE'S NO DANGER AT ALL. THAT'S WHY WE HAVE TO REMAIN DISCREET: WE'LL LAND QUIETLY AND PLAY TOURISTS...

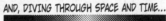

READY FOR THE LAST JUMP?

READY...

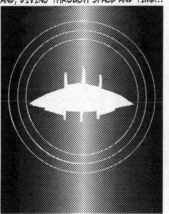

AND, DIVING THROUGH SPACE AND TIME...

... VALERIAN AND LAURELINE'S SHIP MATERIALISES IN A REMOTE CORNER OF THE SYRTIAN SPACEPORT.

SOON...

... VALERIAN AND LAURELINE LEAVE THE SPACEPORT UNIMPEDED AND, ALONGSIDE OTHER TRAVELLERS, HEAD TOWARDS THE CAPITAL.

5A

EVERYTHING'S GOING WELL SO FAR.

YEAH... I'M NOT SURPRISED... MOST SPECIES HERE ARE HUMANOID—WE CAN LOSE OURSELVES IN THE CROWD!

FORTUNATELY, THEY ALSO WEAR ALL KINDS OF OUTFITS! WE'RE BLENDING RIGHT IN...

WHAT A WONDERFUL MARKET! LOOK, IT'S THE JEWELLER'S ALLEY! LET'S GO HAVE A LOOK...

... I HAVE SOME GOLD WITH ME, AND I SAW THAT THEY ACCEPT IT AS CURRENCY HERE.

OH, COME ON! YOU'RE NOT GOING TO START BUYING STUFF, ARE YOU?... FINE...

5B

BRRR... ALL THESE JEWELS YOU STICK ON YOUR SKIN ARE GORGEOUS, BUT I DON'T REALLY FEEL LIKE GOING AROUND WITH CRITTERS ALL OVER ME...

OH, VALERIAN! LOOK!

A WATCH... IT LOOKS VERY OLD. WHAT LOVELY DECORATIONS.

YES... STRANGE... I'VE SEEN VERY SIMILAR ONES AT THE PRE-ATOMIC MUSEUM OF GALAXITY. SO, DO YOU LIKE IT?

5C

YOU'RE SWEET TO BUY IT FOR ME... SMOOCH... IT WORKS, YOU KNOW!

BAH... MISSION EXPENSES! LET'S CHECK OUT THAT GATHERING OVER THERE.

WHAT'S GOING ON?

IS THIS THE FIRST TIME YOU'VE COME TO SYRTE? THEN PAY ATTENTION... THIS IS ONE OF THE MOST FAMOUS OF THE ENLIGHTENEDS. TODAY, HE'S AGREED TO ANSWER QUESTIONS...

... LOOK, A RICH MERCHANT FROM PLANET FLUGIL IS COMING TO CONSULT HIM.

MIGHTY ENLIGHTENED! I CALL UPON YOUR MUNIFICENCE AND BEG AN ANSWER TO THIS QUESTION: WILL I LIVE LONG ENOUGH TO SEE MY BUSINESS PROSPER UNTIL IT IS THE MOST SUCCESSFUL IN THE FIELD THAT IS MINE?

IN THE SILENCE OF THE ATTENTIVE CROWD, A VOICE SOON ECHOES, DEEP IF SLIGHTLY MUFFLED...

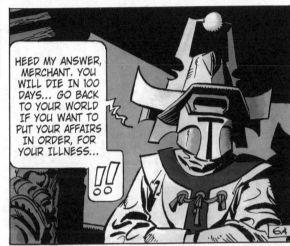

HEED MY ANSWER, MERCHANT. YOU WILL DIE IN 100 DAYS... GO BACK TO YOUR WORLD IF YOU WANT TO PUT YOUR AFFAIRS IN ORDER, FOR YOUR ILLNESS...

SUDDENLY, TO EVERYONE'S SURPRISE, THE ENLIGHTENED STOPS, AND...

YOUNG WOMAN! COME NEAR!

WHAT'S GOING ON?

THE ENLIGHTENEDS NEVER SPEAK TO THE COMMON PEOPLE DIRECTLY...

COME NEAR!!!

WHO... ME?!

YES, YOU! WHERE DID YOU FIND THIS OBJECT?...

WELL... HERE! I JUST BOUGHT IT FROM THE MARKET BECAUSE I LIKED IT, AND...

WHAT IS THE PURPOSE OF THIS... ORNAMENT?

TELLING TIME, OF COURSE! THERE'S NOTHING SPECIAL ABOUT THAT!

HEARING THESE WORDS, THE CROWD AROUND LAURELINE BURSTS OUT LAUGHING, WHILE THE ENLIGHTENED TURNS AWAY WITHOUT A FURTHER WORD AND HURRIES OFF TOWARDS THE PALACE...

BUT... WHAT DID I SAY?...

SHUT UP AND LET'S VAMOOSE! WE MUST HAVE BLUNDERED SOMEHOW, BUT I DON'T KNOW HOW.

TELLING TIME! HA! HA! HA!

THAT GIRL'S CRAZY...

DID YOU SEE? THE ENLIGHTENED WAS OFFENDED BY HER IMPERTINENCE. HE'S LEAVING...

A SHORT WHILE LATER...

I CAN'T WAIT TO GET BACK TO THE SPACEPORT. NIGHT FALLS QUICKLY ON SYRTE, AND I HAVE THIS FEELING THAT WE'RE BEING FOLLOWED...

FOLLOWED BY WHOM? FOR WHAT REASON? THAT WATCH BUSINESS IS JUST STUPID!

7A

DO YOU SEE THOSE TWO BOATS?... THEY'VE BEEN BEHIND US FOR A GOOD LONG WHILE... WE HAVE TO LOSE THEM!

BOATMAN! TAKE THE CANAL TO THE RIGHT, QUICKLY!

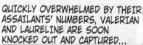

7B

BOM

AND IN THE THICK SYRTIAN NIGHT, A CONFUSED STRUGGLE BEGINS...

QUICKLY OVERWHELMED BY THEIR ASSAILANTS' NUMBERS, VALERIAN AND LAURELINE ARE SOON KNOCKED OUT AND CAPTURED...

7C

10

IN THE MORNING...

OH, MY HEAD... WHERE ARE WE?

ON A SOLAR-POWERED VESSEL. WE'RE ABOUT TO SET SAIL...

... THROUGH EVER MORE ABUNDANT VEGETATION.

INDEED, THE SHIP SOON BEGINS TO PICK UP SPEED. WITH THE SUNS HIGH OVER THE HORIZON, ITS SAILS FULLY DEPLOYED, IT RACES OVER THE CANALS OF SYRTE...

MUCH LATER, AS A GUARD UNTIES VALERIAN AND LAURELINE...

THESE GUARDS ARE MUTE. NOT MUCH CHANCE OF LEARNING WHAT WE CAN EXPECT FROM THEM...

AND, UNDER CLOSE WATCH...

... CROSSING THE GANGWAY JUST LOWERED TO THE QUAY...

VALERIAN! AN ISOLATED TEMPLE! LIKE THE ONES THE AUTOMATIC PROBES LOCATED AND REPORTED...

HMM... ALL WE KNOW IS THAT THE ENLIGHTENEDS LIVE THERE. WELL, LOOKS LIKE WE'RE ABOUT TO LEARN MORE...

... THE SMALL GROUP ENTERS THE ENLIGHTENEDS' SANCTUARY.

WITH A SIMPLE GESTURE, ONE OF THE GUARDS ACTIVATES THE MECHANISM THAT OPENS THE MASSIVE FRONT DOOR.

... WHILE THE DOOR CLOSES BEHIND THEM...

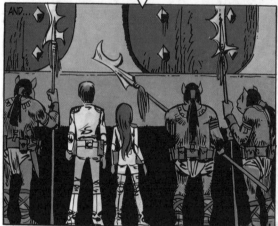

... PUSHED FORWARD BY THE GUARDS...

... VALERIAN AND LAURELINE REACH THE TOP OF THE STAIRS.

PFFF... I BET SOMEONE'S ABOUT TO ASK ME FOR THE TIME AGAIN...

YOU AND YOUR WATCH! IT'S PROBABLY BECAUSE OF IT THAT WE'RE HERE...

AFTER WAITING IN SILENCE...

... THE QUESTION I'M ABOUT TO ASK YOU, YOUNG WOMAN, IS NOT WHAT YOU'RE EXPECTING. BESIDES, I ALREADY KNOW THE ANSWER TO IT. **ARE YOU FROM EARTH?**

WAY TO GO, LAURELINE! A FINE MESS SHE'S GOT US INTO...

SMART, VALERIAN. TALK ABOUT A COVERT MISSION...

DON'T DENY IT! THIS WATCH, AND THE FACT THAT YOU KNOW ITS PURPOSE, HAVE BETRAYED YOU...

HA HA! YOU'D HAVE TO BE AN EARTHLING TO BUY SUCH AN OBJECT. YOU'D HAVE TO BE UNAWARE THAT ALL INHABITANTS OF THE SYRTIAN SYSTEM HAVE AN INNATE, PERFECT SENSE OF TIME...

WE DON'T KNOW WHY YOU CAME TO SYRTE. BUT WE'LL SOON FIND OUT... WE'RE ALREADY INSPECTING YOUR SPACESHIP...

YOU'LL NEVER BE ABLE TO GET INSIDE OUR SHIP. I SET THE SAFETY LOCK FOR SELF-DESTRUCT!

BE SILENT! HOW VERY MUCH LIKE EARTHLINGS. THEIR PRIDE, THEIR OBSTINACY, THEIR FOLLY! **ACCURSED RACE!** OUR VENGEANCE WILL BE TERRIBLE!!!

VENGEANCE?... BUT WHY? WE COME IN PEACE...

THAT'S ENOUGH! YOU WILL REMAIN HERE AS PRISONERS. NO ONE WILL EVER NOTICE YOUR DISAPPEARANCE. WE STILL NEED YOU FOR THE MOMENT; AFTERWARDS...

AFTER THESE OMINOUS WORDS, THE ENLIGHTENED VANISHES INTO THE SHADOWS, WHILE THE THICK BLAST DOOR BEGINS TO DESCEND...

ALL OR NOTHING, LAURELINE!!!

AND, SCRAPING THROUGH...

... VALERIAN AND LAURELINE FIND THEMSELVES IN DARKNESS.

ON THE OTHER SIDE, THE GUARDS SEEM TO BE IN THE GRIP OF EXTREME INDECISION, AS IF SCARED AT THE IDEA OF ENTERING THE ENLIGHTENEDS' DEMESNE TO PURSUE THE FUGITIVES...

WHAT DO WE DO NOW?

ANYTHING EXCEPT STAY HERE. NO DOUBT THE GUARDS WILL RAISE THE ALARM SOON! LET'S HEAD TOWARDS THAT LIGHT, THERE...

NO ONE!

AN ENGINE ROOM!!!

BY THE GALAXY!!! THESE TEMPLES ARE ACTUALLY POWER PLANTS!

FURTHER ON...

LABORATORIES NOW! AND RATHER ADVANCED, IT WOULD SEEM...

YES... THEY USE RELIGION AS A FRONT, BUT IT LOOKS LIKE THE ENLIGHTENEDS HAVE COMPLETE CONTROL OVER SYRTE'S SCIENTIFIC EQUIPMENT...

THE STRANGE THING IS THAT EVERYTHING SEEMS ABANDONED! LOOK AT THESE DEVICES... NO ONE'S TOUCHED THEM FOR YEARS... MAYBE EVEN CENTURIES...

THE MACHINERY IS PROBABLY STILL WORKING, THANKS TO SOME SELF-REPAIR SYSTEMS. BUT NOTHING ELSE SEEMS TO BE IN USE... WELL, ANYWAY, WE'LL WORRY ABOUT THAT LATER...

14

THE IMPORTANT THING FOR THE MOMENT IS TO GET OUT OF HERE. THERE MUST BE SOME AIRCRAFT SOMEWHERE... I DOUBT THE ENLIGHTENEDS ONLY USE SOLAR-POWERED SHIPS...

THEN LET'S GO BACK TO THE POWER PLANT. IF THERE ARE PLANES IN HERE, THAT'S WHERE THEY MUST RECHARGE.

INDEED, A LITTLE LATER...

YOU WERE RIGHT, KIDDO!

HMM... PRETTY STANDARD SETUP, FROM THE NUCLEAR ENGINE TO THE EJECTOR SEAT. I SHOULD BE ABLE TO HANDLE IT...

VALERIAN!

THE GUARDS!!! THEY'VE GONE AROUND! TAKE OFF! THEY'RE ALMOST ON TOP OF US...

HURRY!

TAKE OFF, TAKE OFF!!! EASY FOR YOU TO SAY... I'VE FOUND EVERYTHING EXCEPT THE IGNITION!

THIS ONE?!?

THIS ONE?... NAH...

HEY!!

VALERIAN! THE WALL!!! WATCH IT!!!

UNDER THE—FORTUNATELY—ERRATIC FIRE OF THE GUARDS, VALERIAN SOMEHOW MANAGES...

... TO TAKE HIS PLANE THROUGH THE EXIT...

... BEFORE RACING AWAY JUST ABOVE THE FOREST...

OW... A TAD ON THE ROUGH SIDE TODAY, PILOT!...

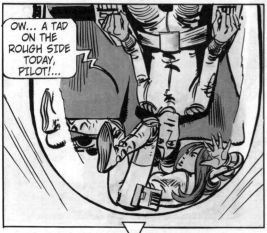

HAHA!... COME ON, STRAIGHTEN UP! FASTEN YOUR SEATBELT—AND CHECK TO SEE IF WE'RE BEING FOLLOWED...

WELL?

THERE ARE TWO JETS PURSUING US!

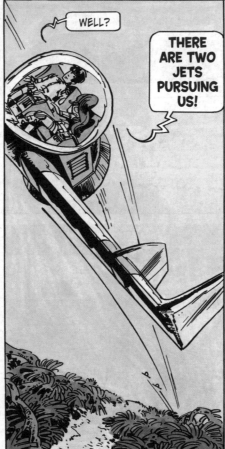

SECONDS TICK BY...THE SYRTIAN AIRCRAFT INEXORABLY CLOSE IN ON VALERIAN...

I CAN'T SHAKE THEM... I DON'T KNOW EVERY-THING THIS BIRD CAN DO... HANG ON... THAT STORM FORMATION OVER THERE?! MAYBE I'LL BE ABLE TO LOSE THEM IN THE CLOUDS...

16

THE EJECTOR SEAT!!! IT'S OUR LAST CHANCE... WE'RE BAILING OUT!

AND, JUST BEFORE THE OUT-OF-CONTROL AIRCRAFT SLAMS INTO A WALL OF ICE...

FINALLY, THE COCKPIT REACHES THE GROUND...

GOOD GRIEF... WE GOT OFF LIGHTLY ON THIS ONE!

YES... NOW I UNDERSTAND WHY OUR PURSUERS TURNED BACK...

THE SYRTIAN WEATHER SYSTEM IS FULL OF SURPRISES. JUST LIKE THE LACK OF WIND, I IMAGINE THESE SUDDEN ICE STORMS ARE THE CONSEQUENCE OF SOME SORT OF ELECTROSTATIC PHENOMENON. SO COLD...

LET'S WALK... OR WE'RE GOING TO FREEZE TO DEATH HERE...

HOLD ME; I'M COLD...

VALERIAN AND LAURELINE BEGIN A LOW MARCH OVER THE FROZEN TERRAIN, COVERED WITH CRUNCHY ROST HERE, SLIPPERY AS A MIRROR THERE...

BUT SOON, AS SWIFTLY AS THE STORM'S ICY COLD HAD COME, THE CLOUDS DISPERSE AND SYRTE'S TWIN BLAZING SUNS REAPPEAR...

IN AN INSTANT, A STRANGE AERIAL VEGETATION SPRINGS FORTH FROM MILLIONS OF SPORES SUSPENDED IN THE ATMOSPHERE...

DRUNK WITH SMELLS AND COLOURS, VALERIAN AND LAURELINE BARELY NOTICE AS THE THIN CRUST OF ICE BEGINS TO CRACK BELOW THEIR FEET...

HOW WONDERFUL THIS IS, VALERIAN... CAN YOU FEEL THE FLOWERS?! HOW SOFTLY THEY BRUSH AGAINST US...

... THE SYRTIAN CLIMATE IS TRULY FULL OF SURPRISES...

WELL! WINTER'S REALLY SHORT ON SYRTE!

YEAH... AT LEAST WE CAN TOUCH BOTTOM HERE...

AS VALERIAN AND LAURELINE STRUGGLE ON THROUGH THE MUDDY WATERS...

HANG IN THERE! SOLID GROUND, STRAIGHT AHEAD!

CRACK

AAHH!

A MARCYAM!

SUDDENLY, A VOLLEY OF BOLTS COMES OUT OF NOWHERE...

... AND STRIKES THE MAGNIFICENT AND TERRIBLE ANIMAL. AS THE BEAST COLLAPSES IN A SERIES OF MASSIVE CONVULSIONS, VALERIAN AND LAURELINE REACH THE SHORE, EXHAUSTED...

JUST THEN, COMING OUT OF A CLUMP OF TREES...

MARCYAM HUNTERS!!!

I'M EXHAUSTED! TOO MUCH HAS HAPPENED TOO QUICKLY!

LATER, AT THE HUNTERS' CAMP...

A GOOD CATCH TODAY! THE MARCYAMS ALWAYS COME OUT OF THEIR WATERHOLES AFTER STORMS. THE POLLEN FROM THE FLOWERS DRIVES THEM MAD...

ARE YOU GOING TO HUNT MORE?...

WE HAVE ENOUGH DRIED SKINS TO SAIL BACK TO THE CAPITAL. IT'S ALMOST TIME FOR THE FESTIVAL OF THE EMPIRE'S AMBASSADORS! A GOOD TIME TO SELL MANY SKINS...

CAN YOU TAKE US THERE?

WE CAN PAY YOU WITH GOLD...

NO! YOU WILL BE OUR GUESTS. WE LEAVE AT DAWN TOMORROW...

18A

DAY AFTER DAY, IN THE STILL AIR, THE SMALL FLOTILLA FOLLOWS THE CANALS THAT CRISSCROSS THE PLANET. THE LUSH FORESTS GIVE WAY TO CULTIVATED FIELDS...

FINALLY...

AND WE'RE BACK IN SYRTE!

YES... WE LOST A LOT OF TIME GETTING BACK HERE! BUT THAT'S NOT SUCH A BAD THING. THAT WAY, THE ENLIGHTENEDS MUST THINK WE'RE DEAD... HOWEVER, WE'RE GOING TO HAVE TO MAKE SURE WE DON'T REPEAT THE MISTAKES WE MADE WHEN WE FIRST ARRIVED...

18B

AT THE FOOT OF THE PALACE'S FORMIDABLE WALLS, VARIOUS BOATS THRONG THE MAIN CANAL, WHICH BUZZES WITH ACTIVITY AS THE TIME OF THE FESTIVAL OF THE AMBASSADORS APPROACHES. AND, AS THE FISHERMEN BUSTLE ABOUT ON THE DOCK AMIDST THE HEADY SCENT OF SPICES, PRECIOUS WOOD ESSENCES AND DRIED SKINS BEING UNLOADED...

WHAT'S YOUR PLAN? MORE COVERT STUFF?

PRECISELY, YOUNG LADY! BEFORE WE DO ANYTHING, WE NEED TO KNOW WHO'S RULING THIS EMPIRE... THE PRINCE OR THE ENLIGHTENEDS? I WANT TO KNOW FOR SURE...

WHAT ABOUT OUR SHIP? YOU ACTUALLY BELIEVE IT'S STILL WAITING FOR US?

OK, THAT'S ENOUGH SARCASM FROM YOU! THERE IS NO WAY WE CAN AFFORD TO SNOOP AROUND A SHIP THAT'S LIKELY UNDER A 'ROUND-THE-CLOCK WATCH! ANYWAY, I'M SURE THE ENLIGHTENEDS HAVEN'T MANAGED TO BREAK IN. THEY WANT IT TOO BADLY TO BLOW IT UP...

THEN... WHAT DO WE DO?

WE'RE GOING TO BUY SOME MORE ELEGANT CLOTHES. AND THEN WE'LL FIND A WAY TO GET INSIDE THE PALACE—BY POSING AS FOREIGN NOBLES INVITED TO THE PARTY.

19 A

A LITTLE LATER...

I MUST SAY, I REALLY LIKE SYRTE! SUCH BEAUTIFUL FABRICS! HOW DO I LOOK?

VERY NICE! COME TAKE A LOOK...

WHAT'S THE RUSH...?

LOOK AT THAT PROCESSION OVER THERE... THIS IS THE PERFECT OPPORTUNITY TO INFILTRATE THE PALACE...

... WE'LL MERGE WITH THAT GROUP OF VISITORS...

19 B

TRY TO LOOK REGAL, OK?... WE HAVE TO IMPRESS THE GUARDS!

YEAH, RIGHT!!!

BUT...

RATS. SO MUCH FOR THAT PLAN...

THE GUARDS MUST HAVE SOME TRICK TO IDENTIFY AUTHORISED VISITORS... THAT MACHINE...

CORRECT! IT'S AN AUTOMATIC DECODER, AND EVERY AMBASSADOR MUST PRESENT HIS PERSONAL SEAL TO IT...

I DID TRY TO FORGE SOME FOR MY OWN USE... BUT IT DIDN'T WORK...

THE MERCHANT FROM EARLIER...

WHAT...

DON'T BE ALARMED! YOU'RE NOT THE FIRST ONES TO BUY CEREMONIAL CLOTHING OFF ME IN AN ATTEMPT TO ENTER THE PALACE. IT'S JUST THAT IT'S A BAD IDEA! IF YOU REALLY WANT TO GET IN, WHY DON'T YOU FOLLOW ME OVER THERE...

23

ACCESS TO THE PALACE WASN'T ALWAYS SO DIFFICULT. BUT NOW, THE RULES ARE SO STRICT THAT EVEN FOOD AND LUXURY ITEMS ARE HOISTED UP THE WALLS LIKE THAT... THEY'RE AFRAID OF PRYING EYES UP THERE...

WHO ARE YOU TO SPEAK IN SUCH A WAY?

I'M ELMIR, HUMBLE MERCHANT OF SYRTE—AT YOUR SERVICE!... AND I HAVE AN OFFER FOR YOU. AFTER NIGHTFALL, I CAN HELP YOU ENTER THE PALACE WITH A SHIPMENT OF SCHAMIRS. IN EXCHANGE...

... I WANT SOME INFORMATION ON THE ENLIGHTENEDS! FOR VARIOUS REASONS, I'D RATHER CALL UPON STRANGERS SUCH AS YOURSELVES. IF YOU MANAGE TO EXIT THE PALACE AGAIN—AND THAT PART IS YOUR PROBLEM—YOU CAN FIND ME IN BLACK STREET. IF YOU BRING ME ANY INFORMATION, I'LL BE ABLE TO HELP YOU AGAIN...

WELL, I'LL BE... COULD IT BE A TRAP...? IT'D BE A CRUDE ONE...

WHERE ARE THE ENLIGHTENEDS?

IN THE OTHER WING OF THE MAIN BUILDING, ACROSS FROM THE PRINCE'S HUGE CHAMBERS, IT IS SAID. I'D LIKE TO KNOW EXACTLY WHAT'S GOING ON THERE... WHAT MACHINES THEY POSSESS... IN SHORT, ANYTHING AND EVERYTHING OF INTEREST. SO...?

ALL RIGHT! YOU HAVE A DEAL...

A LITTLE LATER, IN THE GROWING DARKNESS...

BE CAREFUL NOT TO LET THE SCHAMIRS FULLY CLOSE OVER YOU! THEIR HYPNOTIC FUMES WOULD MAKE YOU FORGET WHO YOU ARE... GOOD LUCK. AND REMEMBER: ELMIR, MERCHANT, BLACK STREET...

AND...

THERE... WE JUST HAVE TO WAIT NOW...

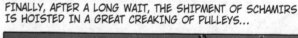

FINALLY, AFTER A LONG WAIT, THE SHIPMENT OF SCHAMIRS IS HOISTED IN A GREAT CREAKING OF PULLEYS...

AFTER A ROUGH LANDING...

... THE TRIP ENDS IN AN ENORMOUS STOCKROOM. STRUGGLING TO BREATHE, AND FIGHTING THE CLOYING INTOXICATION THAT SPREADS THROUGH HIM, VALERIAN WAITS. AS HE GAZES AT THE DISTANT LIGHT OF A TORCH, HE LOSES ALL NOTION OF TIME...

... UNTIL, REASSURED BY THE SILENCE...

LAURELINE... WHERE ARE YOU?

BY SPACE!!! THIS BROKEN SHELL UNDER THE OTHERS MUST HAVE BEEN HERS. WHAT HAPPENED TO HER?... HYPNOTISED, MAYBE...

WHERE DO THESE STAIRS LEAD?... MUSIC... SOUNDS LIKE A PARTY... MAYBE SHE WENT THIS WAY, UNAWARE... I'M GOING...

IT'S A GRANDIOSE SIGHT THAT GREETS VALERIAN AT THE TOP OF THE STAIRS. AMONG THE RUSTLE OF CONVERSATIONS, HE WALKS UNIMPEDED THROUGH GROUPS OF GUESTS, SURROUNDED BY PERFUMES, SOUNDS, AND COLOURS UNKNOWN TO EARTH...

SUCH LUXURY!... LOOK AT THOSE HANGING LODGES...

THIS PALACE MUST BE CHOCK-FULL OF HI-TECH FACILITIES TO MAKE ALL THIS POSSIBLE...

A KHAMAR NECTAR, TRAVELLER?...

ER... WITH PLEASURE...

YOU LOOK SURPRISED! COULD IT BE THE FIRST TIME YOU'RE ATTENDING AN IMPERIAL PARTY?...

ER... YOU COULD SAY THAT...

LOOK UP THERE, UNDER THAT CUPOLA. HIS HIGHNESS PRINCE RAMAL IS ENJOYING HIMSELF! HA! HA!...

23A

BUT... BUT... THAT'S...

LAURELINE!!! I'LL BE...! I'M WILLING TO BELIEVE SHE'S HIGH ON SCHAMIR FUMES, BUT STILL... AND WHAT CAN I DO?!

AH! OUR BELOVED PRINCE'S CUPOLA JUST WENT DARK...

... THE PARTY IS OVER, TRAVELLER...

GOODBYE...

ONLY ONE THING TO DO, NOW THAT I'M HERE. TAKE ADVANTAGE OF THE CONFUSION CAUSED BY THE DEPARTING GUESTS TO PAY THE ENLIGHTENEDS A VISIT...

IN THE DYING LIGHTS OF THE NIGHT'S CELEBRATION, AS THE CUPOLAS GO DARK ONE BY ONE, VALERIAN SNEAKS OUT...

ALL CLEAR, BUT I'D BETTER WATCH FOR PATROLS.

23B

ACCORDING TO THE MERCHANT'S DIRECTIONS, THE ENLIGHTENEDS ARE ON THIS SIDE.

WHAT'S THIS LIGHT? AND THIS MUFFLED SOUND?...

A POWER PLANT JUST LIKE IN THE TEMPLE. BUT THIS ONE IS HUGE... PROBABLY THE PALACE'S NERVE CENTRE...

24A

STILL NO ENLIGHTENEDS, EITHER AT THE PARTY OR HERE...

AND FURTHER STILL, AFTER A PATIENT SEARCH...

THAT TOWER OVER THERE... THAT'S PROBABLY IT... WON'T BE EASY TO REACH!

24B

27

WHILE VALERIAN, HIDDEN IN THE SHADOWS, LOOKS UPON THE STRANGE SPECTACLE, THE ENLIGHTENEDS SLOWLY REMOVE THEIR HEAVY HELMETS. WITH SOLEMN GESTURES, ONE OF THEM PREPARES A SLIGHTLY PHOSPHORESCENT BREW, ITS LIGHT ENCROACHING ON THE DARKNESS...

AH, SOME LUCK AT LAST. THEY'RE GATHERED HERE... WHAT ARE THEY DOING?

SUDDENLY, BEFORE DRINKING THE LIQUID THEY HAVE BEEN SERVED, THE ENLIGHTENEDS UTTER IN PERFECT UNISON A PHRASE THAT SEEMS TO BIND THEM IN RITUAL...

SO THAT WE LIVE, AND THAT EARTH DIES!

BUT A SMALL MOVEMENT FROM VALERIAN CAUSES A PORTCULLIS TO SLAM ONTO THE NARROW LEDGE...

CLANG

THERE! SOMEONE!

RATS! AN ELEC- TRONIC SENSOR!

HURRIEDLY PUTTING THEIR HELMETS BACK ON, THE ENLIGHTENEDS ATTACK, AND...

AFTER A SHORT STRUGGLE...

THE EARTHLING WE BELIEVED LOST!

HE WON'T ESCAPE US THIS TIME. TAKE HIM TO THE INTERROGATION ROOM.

LATER...

EVERYTHING IS READY, EARTHLING! YOU WILL START BY GIVING US THE SECRETS OF YOUR SPACESHIP. AND THEN YOU'LL TELL US ABOUT EARTH... AT LENGTH!

I WON'T TELL YOU ANYTHING!

COME, NOW. THERE'S NO SENSE IN RESISTING. THIS MACHINE ISN'T A TORTURE DEVICE. IT JUST MAKES PEOPLE TALK... BEGIN!!

26A

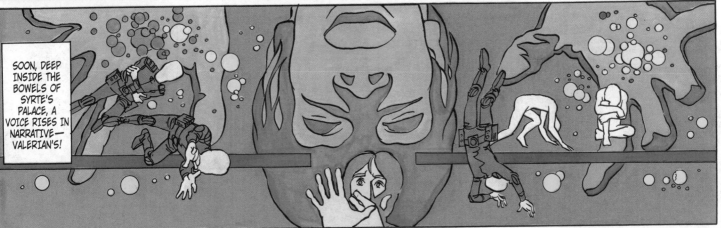

SOON, DEEP INSIDE THE BOWELS OF SYRTE'S PALACE, A VOICE RISES IN NARRATIVE— VALERIAN'S!

THE NEXT MORNING, IN THE NOW-EMPTY ROOM...

HOW HORRIBLE! I DON'T REMEMBER A THING. BUT I KNOW I TALKED... AND WHAT'S BECOME OF LAURELINE?

SUDDENLY, IN THE CORRIDOR...

26B

29

THIS IS THE PRISONER I TOLD YOU ABOUT, MY PRINCE. REMEMBER HOW YOU PROMISED ME YOU'D SET HIM FREE AND GRANT HIM YOUR PARDON...

AHEM, YES, OF COURSE... ER... GUARDS! FREE THIS PRISONER...

HIGHNESS! YOU CANNOT DO THIS. THIS BEING IS DANGEROUS. HE IS A THREAT TO YOUR EMPIRE...

REALLY? ER... IN THAT CASE, PERHAPS WE SHOULD WAIT TO...

PRINCE! ARE YOU NO LONGER THE EMPEROR OF A THOUSAND PLANETS? ARE YOU GOING TO YIELD TO YOUR ADVISORS?!!

ER... NO, NO... OH, THIS MUST END! ALL THIS SHOUTING IS SO TIRESOME. LET THE PRISONER LEAVE WITH THIS GIRL. UNIMPEDED; I PROMISED... GUARDS! ESCORT THEM OUT! AND DO NOT BOTHER ME WITH THIS ANYMORE! I HAVE THE GREAT FESTIVAL OF STELLAR FLOWERS TO ORGANISE FOR TONIGHT, AFTER ALL...

AND WHILE THE PRINCE RETIRES...

VALERIAN IS SET FREE...

UNDER CLOSE WATCH, MARCHING BEFORE THE FROZEN ENLIGHTENEDS...

... THE TWO TERRANS ARE SOON BACK OUTSIDE THE PALACE DOORS...

LET'S PUT SOME DISTANCE BETWEEN THE ENLIGHTENEDS AND US QUICKLY. THEY SEEM PARALYSED FOR THE MOMENT, BUT IT WON'T LAST... AND TELL ME WHAT HAPPENED TO YOU...

CRAZY STORY! IT WAS THAT BLASTED SCHAMIR THAT MADE ME LOSE IT. I WAS STUCK AT THE BOTTOM OF THE HEAP AND COULDN'T BREATHE. IN THE END, I HAD TO BREAK IT TO GET OUT. AFTER THAT, I DON'T REALLY REMEMBER... EXCEPT THAT I ENDED UP INSIDE THE PRINCE'S LODGE. IN THE MORNING, A CALL FROM THE ENLIGHTENEDS INFORMED HIM THAT THEY'D CAPTURED AN IMPORTANT PRISONER...

IT DIDN'T TAKE ME LONG TO FIGURE OUT THAT IT WAS YOU. CONVINCING THE PRINCE WAS CHILD'S PLAY—HE'S A PUSHOVER... BUT HIS ORDERS ARE STILL SACRED. AT LEAST IN PRINCIPLE... THAT'S IT!

PIECE OF CAKE, INDEED! UNFORTUNATELY, I DON'T KNOW WHAT I MIGHT HAVE TOLD THE ENLIGHTENEDS LAST NIGHT. THE ONLY THING THAT'S CERTAIN IS THAT THEY CAN'T HAVE GOT INSIDE THE SHIP YET, SINCE THE LOCK IS SECURED BY A RETINAL SCAN...

ONLY ONE THING TO DO NOW. GET BACK TO ELMIR THE MERCHANT—OUR ONLY ALLY HERE... HEY, KID!! DO YOU KNOW BLACK STREET?

THAT WAY... YOU'VE GOT TO GO DOWN SOME MORE...

SOON, VALERIAN AND LAURELINE ARE WALKING THROUGH A VERITABLE CESSPOOL. LEANING AGAINST WALLS ROTTEN BY THE DAMP, LYING ON THE SLIMY GROUND, THE MISERABLE DREGS OF THE EMPIRE OF A THOUSAND PLANETS SEEM TO WAIT FOR WHO KNOWS WHAT, THEIR EYES EMPTY, UNRESPONSIVE...

SO THIS IS BLACK STREET!!!

YES... JUST LIKE ALL CAPITAL CITIES, SYRTE HAS ITS OWN SEEDY PARTS. LOOK! MANY OF THESE BEINGS HAVE BEEN IRRADIATED; OTHERS HAVE BEEN STRUCK WITH SPACE MADNESS... PERHAPS ONE OF THE POOR DEVILS WILL BE ABLE TO TAKE US TO ELMIR, ANYWAY...

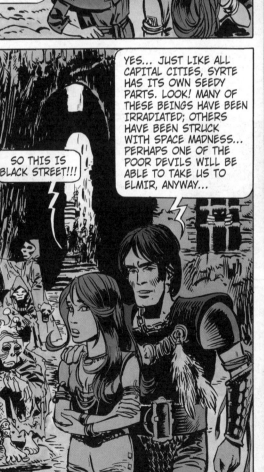

SOME TIME LATER, AFTER A LONG WALK THROUGH DARK, LABYRINTHINE STREETS...

IT'S HERE, LORDS.

THANK YOU. HERE, TAKE THIS.

BAM BAM

WE'RE HERE TO SEE ELMIR THE MERCHANT. TELL HIM WE COME FROM THE PALACE, HE'LL UNDERSTAND.

AFTER A FEW MINUTES...

THIS IS THE GRANDMASTER OF THE MERCHANT GUILD.

?

YES, I DIDN'T TELL YOU THE WHOLE STORY...

... I MUST ALSO CONFESS THAT I'M SORRY TO RECEIVE YOU IN SUCH SQUALOR. BUT THIS IS THE ONLY DISTRICT WHERE THE ENLIGHTENEDS AND THEIR GOONS DON'T DARE GO... YOU'RE SAFE HERE...

BUT DO TELL ME HOW YOU GOT OUT OF THE PALACE WHILE I SHOW YOU TO OUR SECRET MEETING ROOM...

AT THE END OF A MAZE OF STAIRS AND CORRIDORS...

FRIENDS AND COLLEAGUES OF THE GUILD, HERE ARE THE TWO STRANGERS I TOLD YOU ABOUT...

... WE CAN TRUST THEM FOR THE MOMENT. AFTER ALL, THEY HAVE INCURRED THE ENLIGHTENEDS' HATRED, AND THAT'S SUFFICIENT GUARANTEE FOR ME. THEY'LL EXPLAIN WHAT THEY HAVE DISCOVERED. AFTER THAT... WELL, WE'LL SEE IF WE CAN WORK TOGETHER...

ALL RIGHT, LET ME BEGIN...

LATER, AFTER VALERIAN AND LAURELINE HAVE RECOUNTED THEIR ADVENTURES AND ANSWERED MANY QUESTIONS ON THE ENLIGHTENEDS' ACTIVITIES...

HMM... VERY INTERESTING. IT DIDN'T TAKE YOU LONG TO LEARN ALL OF THIS! YOUR INFORMATION CONFIRMS WHAT WE ALREADY SUSPECTED. BUT THERE ARE OTHER THINGS YOU MAY NOT BE AWARE OF...

THOSE ABANDONED LABORATORIES YOU SAW, THE OFF-LIMITS FACTORIES, THE CLOSED UNIVERSITIES... IT'S ALL THE WORK OF THE ENLIGHTENEDS. THEY APPEARED LESS THAN 100 YEARS AGO, AND SYRTE IS ALREADY GOING TO RUIN. KNOWLEDGE IS HUNTED DOWN. RELIGION REPLACES SCIENCE...

OUR SPACESHIPS ARE FALLING TO PIECES. THERE'S NO ONE LEFT TO REPAIR THEM...

AND THE SPACE ROUTES ARE SLOWLY FORGOTTEN BY BADLY TRAINED PILOTS.

BUT THE ENLIGHTENEDS DID MAKE A CONTRIBUTION, DIDN'T THEY?! THEIR POWERS ARE REAL—I'VE SEEN THEM AT WORK...

IT'S TRUE... THEIR MEDICAL AND PSYCHOLOGICAL KNOWLEDGE IS MUCH MORE ADVANCED THAN SYRTE'S, WHERE THIS TYPE OF SCIENCE WAS NEVER OF MUCH INTEREST. IT IS THANKS TO THAT KNOWLEDGE THAT THEY GAINED THEIR HOLD ON THE PEOPLE AND THE NOBILITY...

BUT THEY'VE GAINED THEIR ASCENDANCY PRIMARILY BY RUTHLESSLY ELIMINATING ALL WHO OPPOSE THEM. WITH THE EMPEROR'S UNSPOKEN AGREEMENT, THEY KILL AND KIDNAP WITHOUT MERCY TO TAKE OVER ALL KEY POSITIONS.

THEY'VE EVEN STARTED GOING AFTER OUR SHIPS IN SPACE. MANY PLANETS HAVE STOPPED THEIR COMMERCIAL RELATIONS WITH US BECAUSE OF THEM. IT'S A DISASTER FOR THE GUILD!

NOW YOU KNOW THE ESSENTIALS, AND WE HAVE A PROPOSITION FOR YOU. BUT I MUST FIRST WARN YOU THAT IF YOU BETRAY US, YOU'LL NEVER LEAVE SYRTE ALIVE! SO...

SO IT'S NOT LIKE WE HAVE MUCH CHOICE. ALONE, WE'LL NEVER MANAGE TO EVADE THE ENLIGHTENEDS. THEY MUST BE ON HIGH ALERT...

WHAT'S YOUR OFFER?

HERE'S HOW IT IS... WE'RE PREPARING AN EXPEDITION TO PUSH THE ENLIGHTENEDS OUT OF THEIR BASE. WE RECENTLY RECEIVED SOME INFORMATION, AND WE THINK WE KNOW MORE OR LESS WHERE THEIR LAIR IS. BUT WE LACK WEAPONS AND EXPERIENCE. I'VE SEEN YOUR SHIP... QUITE A MACHINE, NO DOUBT MORE IMPRESSIVE THAN OUR RICKETY OLD TRANSPORTS. WILL YOU TAKE COMMAND OF THE CONVOY WITH ME? SEVERAL PLANETS FEAR SEEING SYRTE REVERT BACK TO THE DARK AGES AND ARE READY TO FOLLOW US. THEY ONLY WAIT FOR OUR SIGNAL TO SEND US THEIR BEST SHIPS. IN EXCHANGE FOR YOUR HELP, WE OFFER YOU PROTECTION AGAINST THE ENLIGHTENEDS AND A WAY TO RETAKE YOUR OWN SHIP. NOT TO MENTION OUR PROMISE THAT YOU CAN LEAVE FREELY ONCE YOUR MISSION IS COMPLETE.

ALL RIGHT, I ACCEPT! WHEN ARE YOU PLANNING TO LEAVE SYRTE?

30A

IN A FEW DAYS. WE JUST NEED TO COMPLETE OUR PREPARATIONS. I'LL GIVE YOU THE DETAILS OF THE PLAN ONCE WE'RE UNDERWAY. IN THE MEANTIME, YOU'D PROBABLY LIKE TO GET SOME REST?

NOT LIKE IT'D BE WISE TO GO OUT FOR A WALK INSTEAD.

AND...

YOUR CHAMBERS! CONSIDER YOURSELF AT HOME... WELL... SO TO SPEAK... BECAUSE... ERM... ACTUALLY, WHERE EXACTLY IS HOME?

TSK, TSK... DON'T BE TOO CURIOUS, ELMIR!

DON'T WORRY, LAURELINE. I'M SURE THE GUILD UNDERSTANDS THE NEED FOR SECRECY IN BUSINESS MATTERS...

THREE DAYS LATER...

OH, OH! THE PEACEFUL MERCHANTS OF THE GUILD, NOW TURNED MIGHTY WARRIORS!

WHAT CAN I SAY? I'D MUCH RATHER BE RUNNING MY BUSINESS IN PEACE. BUT I DON'T EVEN GO OUT WITHOUT BODYGUARDS ANYMORE. THE ENLIGHTENEDS HAVE SCOURED THE ENTIRE CITY TO FIND YOU, AND THE SPACEPORT IS FULL OF SPIES.

ANYWAY... WE'RE READY! THE TOUGHEST PART COMES NOW...

HOW ARE YOU GOING TO PROCEED?

WITH THE SIMPLEST PLAN OF ALL: OPENLY AND IN BROAD DAYLIGHT, AS YOU'LL SEE! HA! HA! LET'S GO— THEY'RE WAITING FOR US.

30B

SOON, DOWN IN THE SLUMS OF SYRTE, A MARCH BEGINS. AT EACH CROSSROAD, A NEW CONTINGENT OF GUILD MEMBERS JOINS THE PROCESSION...

ON THE DOCKS, THE CROWD IS EVEN THICKER...

WELL DONE, ELMIR!

NOT BAD, IT'S TRUE... BUT MAKE NO MISTAKE: FLUNKIES OF THE ENLIGHTENEDS ARE LYING IN WAIT EVERYWHERE. KEEP YOUR HEADS DOWN FOR THE CROSSING...

WHEN THEY ARRIVE AT THE SPACEPORT, IT IS AN ENORMOUS CROWD THAT ESCORTS VALERIAN AND LAURELINE TO THEIR SHIP. UNABLE TO DO A THING, THE GUARDS WATCH FROM THE SIDELINES...

THAT'S IT! WE'RE THROUGH!

YES. AND THE THREE SHIPS IMMEDIATELY AROUND YOURS WILL COME WITH US. THEY BELONG TO THE GUILD. OTHERS WILL JOIN US ALONG THE WAY.

EVERYTHING LOOKS INTACT; THEY COULDN'T GET PAST THE LOCK. GET IN, QUICK!

I HAVE AN OLD MAP OF THE SYRTIAN SYSTEM WITH ME. ONE OF THE FEW COMPLETE ONES...

AND SOON, IN SYRTE'S SERENE SKY...

... MOST OF THE EMPIRE'S ARCHIVES HAVE VANISHED IN THE PAST FEW YEARS—WHAT A COINCIDENCE—TO THE POINT THAT THERE ARE MANY PLANETS NOW FORGOTTEN ALTOGETHER... FOR THE MOMENT, HEAD TOWARDS THE CONSTEL-LATION OF THE EAGLE. I'LL GIVE YOU THE COURSE CORRECTIONS LATER, ONCE OUR CONVOY IS ASSEMBLED.

UNDERSTOOD. LET'S GO... LAURELINE, CALL THE OTHERS AND GIVE THEM THE FOLLOW-ING VECTORS...

EVERYWHERE WITHIN THE EMPIRE OF A THOUSAND PLANETS, NEWS OF THE EXPEDITION'S DEPARTURE REACHES THOSE WHO HAVE BEEN WAITING FOR THAT MOMENT, SOMETIMES FOR YEARS. IN THE SECRET CODE OF THE MERCHANT GUILD, RENDEZVOUS POINTS IN SPACE ARE SET...

FROM MURMYL, HOME OF THE SYSTEM'S GREATEST ARCHITECTS...

FROM THE FOREST PLANET GLAM, WITH ITS FREEDOM-LOVING POPU-LATION...

FROM THE POWERFUL INDUS-TRIAL CENTRE OF MINTEL...

COME IN... THE GUILD IS CALLING ITS REPRESENTATIVE ON SIMIUS... JOIN US AT THE AGREED-UPON COORDINATES...

FROM EVERY WORLD WHERE THE YOKE OF THE ENLIGHTENEDS HAS BROUGHT ITS LOT OF VICTIMS, BROKEN A CULTURE OR SMOTHERED A TRADE, PEOPLE TAKE OFF TO JOIN THE CRUSADE...

32

A POWERFUL CONVOY IS SLOWLY PUT TOGETHER. ALMOST IMPERCEPTIBLY, IT STRAYS OFF THE TRADE ROUTES AND PLUNGES INTO DEEP SPACE. HOURS PASS BY SLOWLY...

IN VALERIAN'S SHIP, WHERE—AT ELMIR'S REQUEST—EVERYTHING IS READY TO FACE POSSIBLE COMBAT...

MY FRIENDS, WE'RE NEARING OUR OBJECTIVE. THE TIME HAS COME TO EXPLAIN OUR PLAN TO YOU. LOOK AT THE MAP: THIS IS SLOHM, A DUSTBALL ASTEROID CHARTED BY OUR SCOUTS MANY MILLENNIA AGO, AND COMPLETELY ABANDONED SINCE...

A POOR WRETCH WHO WAS BEING KEPT PRISONER THERE BY THE ENLIGHTENEDS MANAGED TO ESCAPE BY HIDING ABOARD ONE OF THEIR CRAFT... BEFORE HE DIED, SHORTLY AFTER REACHING SYRTE, HE REVEALED THAT A GIGANTIC SHIPWRECK ON THE SURFACE SERVED AS THE ENLIGHTENEDS' BASE. FROM THERE, THEY CONTROL ALL THEIR EMISSARIES ON OTHER PLANETS.

THEY ALSO ESTABLISHED SOME SORT OF LABOUR CAMP. THE PRISONERS, WATCHED BY ARMED GUARDS, SEEM TO BE WORKING TO SUSTAIN THEIR MASTERS...

AND YOU WANT TO STRIKE AT THE HEAD, TO DEPRIVE THE ENLIGHTENEDS SCATTERED AROUND THE SYSTEM OF A RALLYING POINT! RISKY, BUT IF IT WORKS...

SO, IN OTHER WORDS, WE'RE FLYING STRAIGHT INTO THE LION'S DEN!! BUT, SURELY SLOHM IS WELL DEFENDED?

NO DOUBT... WHICH IS PRECISELY WHY THE CONVOY WILL MAKE A TEMPTING TARGET FOR THE ENLIGHTENEDS' FORCES... AS OUR DEPARTURE WAS NOT IN THE LEAST DISCREET, I'M SURE THEY'LL MAKE A PREEMPTIVE STRIKE—BOTH TO NEUTRALISE OUR SHIPS AND TO GET THEIR HANDS ON YOU AGAIN. THE FIRST BATTLE WILL TAKE PLACE IN SPACE... OR MORE ACCURATELY, IN SPACE/TIME!... I KNOW YOUR SHIP CAN MAKE THE JUMP, WHICH GIVES IT AN UNMATCHED ADVANTAGE...

HOW DO YOU KNOW THIS?...

EASY TO FIGURE OUT. TO START WITH, YOU'RE THE FIRST STRANGERS TO VISIT THE SYRTIAN SYSTEM—AS YOUR DISASTROUS IGNORANCE OF OUR CUSTOMS PROVES. BESIDES, WHAT ELSE WOULD ALL THESE EXTRA INSTRUMENTS ON YOUR BRIDGE BE FOR?

TOUCHÉ... I WAS ABOUT TO TELL YOU, ANYWAY... I THINK IT'S ALSO TIME FOR US TO TELL YOU WHERE WE COME FROM...

NO NEED! BACK WHEN THERE WAS STILL SCIENTIFIC RESEARCH DONE ON SYRTE, OUR ASTRONOMERS HAD QUITE THE REPUTATION... I DABBLED IN SUCH THINGS MYSELF IN MY YOUTH. YOU COME FROM THE SOL SYSTEM! JUDGING BY YOUR PHYSICAL CONFIGURATION, I'D EVEN SAY THE THIRD PLANET...

TOUCHÉ AGAIN! BUT HOW DID YOU...

THE TIMEPIECE, OF COURSE! I WAS IN THE CROWD WHEN YOU FIRST ENCOUNTERED AN ENLIGHTENED. I ASKED A FEW QUESTIONS OF THE COLLEAGUE WHO SOLD YOU THE ITEM IN QUESTION. I LEARNED A LOT ABOUT ITS ORIGIN...

AND IT'S THE STRANGEST THING: THAT WATCH, AS YOU CALL IT, WAS EXCHANGED FOR SOME JEWELLERY BY AN ENLIGHTENED... WHICH WOULD TEND TO MEAN THAT...

VALERIAN! DISTRESS CALL FROM THE GLAM SHIP! THEY'RE UNDER ATTACK!!!

HERE WE GO... THE TRAP IS SPRUNG—EVEN EARLIER THAN WE THOUGHT...

YES... THE QUESTION NOW IS: WHO'S CAUGHT IN IT?

34A

IN AN INSTANT, THE ENLIGHTENEDS' SHIPS APPEAR OUT OF NOWHERE AND OPEN FIRE ON THE CONVOY WITH DEADLY ACCURACY. BUT THEIR TARGETS, ON ALERT, RETURN FIRE WITH EQUAL RUTHLESS-NESS. IN THE BLAZE OF THERMAL SHIELDS, IN THE CHAOS OF CRISSCROSSING VIDEO CALLS...

... VALERIAN, WHO HAS TAKEN THE HELM OF HIS SHIP, IS ABOUT TO JOIN THE FIGHT...

I MUST WARN YOU, ELMIR! THE FIRST JUMP IS ALWAYS A SERIOUS SHOCK—AND WE'RE ABOUT TO CHAIN SEVERAL HERE. EVEN LAURELINE AND I CAN'T BE CERTAIN OF SURVIVING IT...

I HAVE FAITH! THE FUTURE OF SYRTE IS AT STAKE!

THEN, DIVING INTO SPACE/TIME...

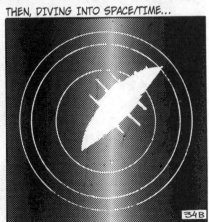

34B

... THE TERRAN SHIP MATERIALISES IN QUICK SUCCESSION AT KEY POINTS OF THE BATTLE. IN A FEW MILLIONTHS OF A SECOND, IT CONDUCTS A SERIES OF SPACE/TIME JUMPS WITH PERFECT PRECISION...

IN THE SILENCE OF SPACE, THE INESCAPABLE SALVOES OF ITS MOLECULAR CANNONS CREATE A SINGLE, BLINDING FLASH OF LIGHT... INSTANTLY TURNING THE TIDE OF THE BATTLE IN FAVOUR OF THE GUILD.

FLOATING ADRIFT AMONG THE CHARRED REM-NANTS OF THE ENLIGHTENEDS' VESSELS, VALERIAN'S SHIP IS BROUGHT TO A STOP BY HIS EXHAUSTED PILOT. AS SUDDENLY AS IT HAD BEGUN, THE BATTLE IS OVER. AND WHILE, IN THE DISTANCE, THE PARTLY-DECIMATED CONVOY CONTINUES ON ITS WAY...

... I'M SO DEADLY TIRED... FEEL LIKE I'VE JUST AGED A CENTURY... WHAT ABOUT LAURELINE?... ELMIR?...

PHEWWW... YOU TOOK SOME INSANE RISKS... HOW'S ELMIR?...

HE'S STARTING TO COME TO. CALL THE OTHER SHIPS AND TELL THEM TO HEAD STRAIGHT FOR SLOHM. WE HAVE TO MAINTAIN THE ELEMENT OF SURPRISE...

ABOVE SLOHM, A GHOST CONVOY PREPARES TO LAND...

SOON...

WE'RE NEARING SLOHM... I LOCATED THE LABOUR CAMP AND THE ENLIGHTENEDS' VESSEL. NO SIGN OF ANY REACTION YET... THAT'S WEIRD...

HMM... WE'LL LAND SOME DISTANCE FROM THE CAMP. ASK THE CONVOY TO FLY IN CLOSE FORMATION AROUND US, AND SWITCH ON THE CLOAKING FIELD. WE'LL BE PROTECTED FROM SIGHT AND RADAR FOR THE LANDING...

AND IT'S THE LANDING AT LAST. IN ABSOLUTE SILENCE, THE INVISIBLE SHIPS TOUCH DOWN IN THE MIDDLE OF A DESOLATE CRATER...

SWITCH OFF THE CLOAKING FIELD, LAURELINE. IT'S SUCKING OUR ENERGY RESERVES DRY! BUT IT WAS WORTH IT. INSIDE THIS CRATER, WE SHOULD REMAIN UNDETECTED... ELMIR! TELL YOUR FRIENDS THAT THEY CAN GET OUT...

SHORTLY AFTERWARDS...

WHAT A DREADFUL PLACE! THOSE HILLS LOOK LIKE LIVING BEINGS...

THE GEOLOGISTS WHO EXPLORED SLOHM LONG AGO SAID THAT THESE ARE THE ANCIENT INHABITANTS OF THE ASTEROID. THEY'RE SLOWLY MERGING WITH THE SURFACE, FOREVER PARALYSED. LOOK AT THIS LIQUID RUNNING DOWN THE SIDES OF THE ROCK FACES... THEY LOOK LIKE TEARS ROLLING FROM GIGANTIC EYES...

ANYWAY... NOW'S HARDLY THE TIME FOR ROMANTIC NOTIONS! GRAB THESE WEAPONS AND LET'S JOIN THE OTHERS...

374

AFTER REGROUPING QUICKLY, A SMALL BAND SOON ADVANCES BETWEEN THE STRANGE HILLS...

THESE TEARS... IT'S STRANGE; THEY REMIND ME OF SOMETHING— BUT WHAT?...

AFTER ONE LAST RIDGE...

HALT! WE'RE HERE. THERE'S THE LABOUR CAMP. AND IN THE MIDDLE OF IT, THE ENLIGHTENEDS' VESSEL.

37B

LET'S SPLIT UP. WE'RE GOING TO HAVE TO TAKE THE GUARDS BY SURPRISE IF WE WANT TO AVOID CAUSING A MASSACRE OF THE PRISONERS.

VERY WELL. I'LL SPLIT US INTO FOUR GROUPS AND GET THEM INTO POSITION AROUND THE CRATER... YOU'LL GIVE THE SIGNAL TO ATTACK BY FIRING THE FIRST SHOT.

ALL RIGHT. MAKE SURE YOU DON'T GIVE THEM TIME TO FIRE BACK...

IN SMALL GROUPS, THE GUILD'S TROOPS SCATTER THROUGH THE SHADOWS. SILENCE STILL REIGNS OVER THE CAMP, ONLY BROKEN BY THE OCCASIONAL CRACK OF A WHIP OR HOARSE SCREAM WHEN A PRISONER IS TARGETED BY A GUARD. THE POOR WRETCHES CLIMB ONTO RICKETY PLATFORMS TO GATHER THE PHOSPHORESCENT LIQUID THAT FLOWS SPARINGLY DOWN THE ROCK. BUCKETS PASS FROM HAND TO HAND. NOT A WORD IS EXCHANGED, NOT A LAMENT IS HEARD... AN OPPRESSIVE, HOPE-CRUSHING ROUTINE SEEMS TO PERMEATE EVERY GESTURE...

SUDDENLY...

COMPLETE CHAOS SOON OVERTAKES THE ENTIRE CAMP. LEAVING THEIR POSTS NEAR THE ENLIGHTENEDS' VESSEL, MORE GUARDS JUMP INTO THE FRAY— BUT IN VAIN.

HELPED BY THE PRISONERS, WHO HAVE QUICKLY SEIZED ON THE EXTRAORDINARY CHANCE GIVEN TO THEM...

... LED BY VALERIAN AND LAURELINE...

... THE GUILD'S FIGHTERS STORM THE CAMP AND TAKE IT.

SOON AFTER, MORNING COMES TO THE ASTEROID. THE FORMER PRISONERS AND THEIR LIBERATORS STAND BEFORE THE MASSIVE SHIPWRECK ON SLOHM'S SURFACE...

NO REACTION FROM THE ENLIGHTENEDS... THIS IS STRANGE...

FACING THE ENORMOUS, STILL STRUCTURE, THE BESIEGERS ARE GRIPPED BY INDECISION.

WHAT DO WE DO NOW?

HMM... I WONDER WHAT THIS SILENCE CAN MEAN. WE SHOULD GO IN AND SEE...

DON'T GO INSIDE THIS SHIP. EVEN THE GUARDS NEVER DID. THEY SAY IT'S CERTAIN DEATH FOR ANY WHO VENTURE INSIDE...

EARTHLING! WE'RE WAITING FOR YOU ABOARD. YOU ALONE! YOU WILL BE SAFE.

I'M COMING!

WHEN VALERIAN ENTERS THE SPACESHIP, HE IS GREETED BY SCENES OF DESOLATION. ABANDONED HYDROPONICS PLANTATIONS GROWN OUT OF CONTROL...

... HUMAN AND ANIMAL SKELETONS...

... RUINED ENGINES AND GUTTED WALLS...

WHEN HE FINALLY REACHES THE COCKPIT...

HERE I AM... I'M VALERIAN. AND YOU, WHO ARE YOU?

HUMANS, LIKE YOU!... OR, MORE ACCURATELY, WHAT'S LEFT OF THEM!...

GAZE UPON US, SINCE YOU WANT TO KNOW WHAT WE LOOK LIKE!

I... I DON'T UNDERSTAND...

WHEN YOU GET BACK TO EARTH, YOU CAN CONSULT THE ARCHIVES OF THAT NEW CAPITAL YOU SPOKE OF TO OUR BROTHERS AT THE IMPERIAL PALACE... THE GALAXITY THAT SENT YOU... YOU WILL DISCOVER THAT A GIANT SHIP, CARRYING ALL THE HOPES OF THE HUMAN RACE, LEFT THE MOTHER PLANET CENTURIES AGO.

LOOK AT THESE OLD IMAGES; WE'VE KEPT THEM SO AS NOT TO FORGET OUR PAST...

BUT... SEVERAL MISSIONS WERE SENT TO FIND THIS SHIP SINCE THE ADVENT OF THE SPACE/TIME JUMP! IT WAS BELIEVED THAT IT HAD DISAPPEARED WITH ALL HANDS IN SOME SORT OF COSMIC DISASTER...

OUR VESSEL WAS CREWED BY THE BEST SCIENTISTS AT THE TIME. IT WAS SUPPOSED TO SEEK NEW WORLDS TO REPLACE EARTH, WHICH WAS DYING, ITS SURFACE DEVASTATED BY NUCLEAR EXPLOSIONS... I WAS ITS CAPTAIN...

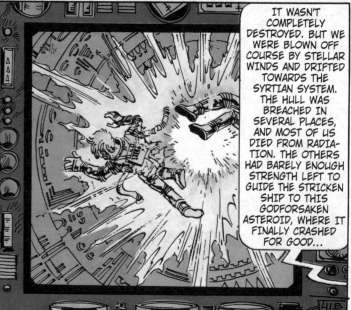

IT WASN'T COMPLETELY DESTROYED. BUT WE WERE BLOWN OFF COURSE BY STELLAR WINDS AND DRIFTED TOWARDS THE SYRTIAN SYSTEM. THE HULL WAS BREACHED IN SEVERAL PLACES, AND MOST OF US DIED FROM RADIATION. THE OTHERS HAD BARELY ENOUGH STRENGTH LEFT TO GUIDE THE STRICKEN SHIP TO THIS GODFORSAKEN ASTEROID, WHERE IT FINALLY CRASHED FOR GOOD...

THOSE WHO WERE LEFT OWED THEIR SURVIVAL TO THE PHOSPHORESCENT TEARS WE COLLECTED FROM SLOHM... OUR EQUIPMENT HAD DETECTED THE PRESENCE OF THIS POWERFUL ANTIDOTE TO THE AILMENTS OF SPACE... OUR DOCTORS TURNED IT INTO A TRUE ELIXIR OF IMMORTALITY.

THAT BREW I SAW THEM DRINK ON SYRTE! SO THIS IS HOW THESE POOR WRETCHES SURVIVED ALL THIS TIME.

THREE CENTURIES PASSED BEFORE WE COULD CAPTURE A SYRTIAN SPACESHIP THAT HAD LANDED ON SLOHM AFTER AN EMERGENCY. THEN, SOME OF US LEFT THIS ACCURSED ROCK TO COLONISE SYRTE. NOW KNOWN AS THE ENLIGHTENEDS, WE FOUNDED A RELIGION AND INFILTRATED THE SYSTEM'S POWER STRUCTURE. ONCE IT WAS COMPLETELY UNDER OUR CONTROL, WE WERE TO USE THE RICHES OF THE EMPIRE TO RETURN TO EARTH IN A POSITION OF STRENGTH.

WHY MOUNT SUCH AN EXPEDITION?

DON'T YOU UNDERSTAND? THE EARTH TURNED US INTO COSMIC MONSTROSITIES!

BEINGS SUSTAINED ONLY BY THE THOUGHT OF TAKING REVENGE AGAINST THEIR MOTHER PLANET!

... IMMORTALS WITHOUT A REASON TO LIVE!

COME BACK TO EARTH! YOU'LL BE TREATED AS HEROES!

IMPOSSIBLE! WE'RE JUST HOMELESS TRASH NOW. AND YET, YOUR ARRIVAL HAD GIVEN RISE TO SUCH HIGH HOPES IN US. WE THOUGHT WE WOULD EXTRACT THE SECRET OF SPACE/TIME TRAVEL FROM YOU. BUT YOU KEPT EVADING US. IN THE END, WE ONLY SUCCEEDED IN LOSING EVERY LAST ONE OF OUR SHIPS IN YESTERDAY'S BATTLE— WE THREW EVERYTHING WE HAD AT YOU...

WE CANNOT COMPETE WITH THE TERRIFYING WEAPONS OF TODAY'S EARTH. AND WE BELONG NEITHER ON OUR WORLD, WHERE WE ARE FORGOTTEN, NOR ON SYRTE, WHERE WE'RE HATED. SO WE'VE MADE OUR DECISION...

WHAT DO YOU MEAN?

IN EXACTLY FIVE MINUTES, THIS WRECK WILL BLOW UP—AND US WITH IT!

TAKE THIS. YOU CAN USE IT AS PROOF OF OUR EXISTENCE WHEN YOU TELL OUR PATHETIC TALE...

THE WATCH WE FOUND IN SYRTE'S MARKET!

42A

INDEED... IT BELONGED TO ONE OF US... TIME, ALWAYS THE OBSESSION OF MEN... GOODBYE NOW, EARTHLING. WE HAVE NOTHING LEFT TO SAY, AND THE SHIP WILL EXPLODE VERY SOON...

AND...

TAKE COVER! IT'S GONNA BLOW!!!

42B

45

A FEW DAYS LATER, AS THE GUILD'S CONVOY IS HEADING BACK TO SYRTE, CARRYING SLOHM'S FORMER PRISONERS...

IT'S ALL OVER, VALERIAN. I CALLED THE REPRESENTATIVES OF THE GUILD THROUGHOUT THE EMPIRE. EVERYWHERE, WHEN THEY HEARD THAT SLOHM HAD FALLEN, THE LAST ENLIGHTENEDS BLEW THEMSELVES UP WITH THEIR TEMPLES. A TERRIBLE END, BUT MAYBE IT HAD TO BE THIS WAY...

NOW THAT THE DANGER IS GONE, EVERYTHING WILL GO BACK TO THE WAY IT WAS... AH! THE MERCHANT GUILD WILL ONCE AGAIN DO GREAT THINGS! THINGS HAPPENED SO FAST, THANKS TO YOUR HELP, VALERIAN... IT'S HARD TO BELIEVE...

YOU'RE RIGHT NOT TO BELIEVE IT TOO EASILY, ELMIR. DO YOU REALLY THINK THINGS WILL REVERT TO WHAT THEY WERE?

43A

WHAT DO YOU MEAN?

I'VE RECEIVED SOME NEWS TOO. WHILE YOU WERE PLACING YOUR CALLS, LAURELINE MANAGED TO CONTACT THE CAPITAL... **THE REVOLUTION HAS BEGUN ON SYRTE!**

THE FISHERMEN, THE FARMERS, THE CRAFTSMEN... THEY'RE STORMING THE PALACE... LONG-FORGOTTEN TEACHERS, EXILED SCIENTISTS HAVE COME OUT OF HIDING TO LEAD THE REVOLT... OTHER PLANETS ARE RISING UP TOO. EVERYWHERE, THE IMPERIAL ARISTOCRACY IS THREATENED...

SERIOUSLY, ELMIR... HOW DO YOU EXPLAIN THE EASE WITH WHICH THE ENLIGHTENEDS TOOK OVER THE EMPIRE? IT WAS BECAUSE IT WAS ALREADY SICK... TOO MANY PARTIES AND WEALTH ON ONE SIDE, TOO MUCH MISERY AND IGNORANCE ON THE OTHER...

THE MERCHANT GUILD THOUGHT IT WAS A VOICE OF REBELLION, BUT IT'S BEEN OVERTAKEN BY THE SUCCESS OF ITS OWN RAID. FEAR OF THE ENLIGHTENEDS WAS THE LOCK THAT KEPT THE IMPERIAL SYSTEM IN PLACE. WHEN YOU REMOVED IT, YOU RELEASED OTHER FORCES...

ERM... I DON'T REALLY MIND, TO BE HONEST. WHATEVER REGIME REPLACES OUR DYNASTY OF HALFWITS, THEY'LL HAVE NEED OF CLEVER PEOPLE... SAY... IF WE LEFT THAT CONVOY OF SLOWPOKES BEHIND AND JUMPED, WE COULD ARRIVE AT SYRTE IMMEDIATELY, COULDN'T WE?...

THEN, WHAT ARE WE WAITING FOR?...

HA, HA... OF COURSE...

AND, DIVING ONCE AGAIN INTO SPACE/TIME...

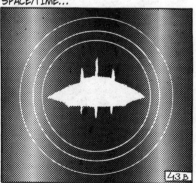

43B

. THE TERRAN SHIP MATERIALISES ‹BOVE SYRTE'S SPACEPORT, WHERE ‹HE BATTLE RAGES...

SOON...

THOSE HOTHEADS ARE AS BAD AS YOU WERE ABOUT GETTING INTO THE PALACE...

... A GOOD THING ELMIR HAS A FEW IDEAS ABOUT HOW TO DO SO DISCREETLY. YOU NEVER KNOW... IT MIGHT BE A GOOD THING TO BE AMONG THE FIRST INSIDE—IN CASE OF PRO-VISIONAL GOVERNMENTS, THAT SORT OF THING, YOU KNOW! GOODBYE, FRIENDS... AND DON'T FORGET: ONCE I'M IN POWER, I'LL BE COMPLE-TELY OPEN TO TRADE RELATIONS BETWEEN EARTH AND SYRTE!!

GOODBYE, ELMIR!

GOOD OLD, CYNICAL ELMIR! I LIKED HIM, THOUGH...

WE'LL SEE HIM AGAIN... NO DOUBT EARTH WILL SEND A LARGE-SCALE MISSION TO SYRTE ONCE WE TURN IN OUR REPORT. BUT, FOR THE MOMENT, THEY DON'T NEED US HERE ANYMORE. WE'RE GOING HOME.

STORY: P. CHRISTIN
DRAWING: J.C. MEZIERES
1970

THE END.

CONVERGENCE OR BORROWING?

CINEBOOK and the authors are delighted to bring you, for the first time, the English version of *The Empire of a Thousand Planets*.

Published in France in 1969 in the weekly comic magazine *Pilote*, *The Empire of a Thousand Planets* is the second story featuring Valerian and Laureline, following *The City of Shifting Waters*. It is the beginning of Mezieres and Christin's heroes' adventures through space and time, with all the promise and all the clumsiness one can expect from a pair of beginners.

L'empire des mille planètes (*The Empire of a Thousand Planets*) was published as a graphic novel in 1971 by Dargaud, who would go on publishing the series for over 40 years. It quickly became very popular in Europe, as it told stories that were outside the frame of *bande dessinée** at the time… and outside the frame of cinema, as "Star Wars" and other memorable science-fiction movies didn't exist yet. Comics and movies have often influenced each other since the beginning of the 20th century. Where Valerian and Laureline are concerned, the similarities are puzzling…

* *Bande dessinée* (or BD): "Drawn strip"—French term for comics or cartoons

Welcome to Alflolol - 1972

Star Wars - 1977

The Land Without Stars - 1972

Return of the Jedi - 1983

The Empire of a Thousand Planets - 1971

The Empire Strikes Back - 1980

The Empire of a Thousand Planets - 1971

Revenge of the Sith - 2005

The Empire of a Thousand Planets - 1971

Revenge of the Sith - 2005

Ambassador of the Shadows - 1975

The Phantom Menace - 2003